garden gnomes broken bones
AND CATACOMBS

ALGO VON LOKI

"As Michael Brueggeman's number one supporter and soon to be wife I felt an obligation to give an overly-positive review of this book containing his adult life's poetry collection. Until I read through it. I now feel an even stronger obligation to the readers, and their loved ones, to warn them about the literary travesty placed appropriately behind a cover showing the most perfect representation of even poorer talent, which hardly seemed possible. After reading this 'poetry?' from cover to cover every day for a month, I still have yet to find a single group of coherent words or letters, for that matter. I would have to say, in all honesty, most of the poems can be described as obvious onomatopoeia solely based on the noises coming from a semi-retarded deaf guy during sudden, nonconsensual anal sex with various sizes of splintered, wooden baseball bats. Purchase at your own risk. Read at your own peril." -ex-finacee Nicole Rehbein.

"All I can say about Garden Gnomes, Broken Bones and Catacombs is this: Although the prose is rather 'rhymey' and quite catchy, it certainly wasn't written by the young man I raised. I am shocked at the irreverence and vulgar words that came from my son's filthy mind. I am so embarrassed that recently I was forced to start using my maiden name to keep from being associated with such a creepy deviant." -Jennifer LANE

"We recently traced an unauthorized access to our mainframe back to your IP address. Any further insurrections into our system traced to your computer will result in legal action. This is a warning to cease and desist all illegal activities on the part of MICHAEL BRUEGGEMAN. Charges will be filed and you will face imprisonment. This will be your only warning." -www.onedirectionmusic.com

Copyright © Michael Brueggeman
Cover Art – D.F. Noble

All rights reserved. No part of this book may be reproduced or transmitted in any form or by any means, electronic or mechanical, including photocopying, recording, or by any information storage and retrieval system, without the written consent of the publisher, except where permitted by law.
Printed in the USA.

www.riotforgestudios.com

Garden Gnomes, Broken Bones & Catacombs

To my aunts, Billie and Angie. Billie showed me exactly where that fine line between genius and insanity truly lies. She regaled us with stories of her relationship with Elvis Presley, to tales of Disneyland being in her backyard. She was a genius and a sweetheart and only ever let us see the fun side of madness. Angie was a woman who came of as misanthropic but in reality was one of the most caring people I've ever known. But she did not suffer liars or bullshit. She told it straight. She never sugar-coated so much as a grapefruit. I will miss these women daily and lament that my son and future children will not know them. But I remain thankful that I got to. Wherever their spirits or energy may be now, if they contain even a fraction of a percent of their respective consciousnesses, that place is much more bright and vibrant for having their presence. They will be missed. But my aim is getting better ;)

we make women bleed

he looks around
looks for lies, lasciviousness
prays to someone else's god
he's not the only one
in this shallow bog
i'm not the only
hunchbacked ghoul
tooling the pools
of festered desire
the only sick lire
in this pyre of doomed lust
trust and betrayal and
sickening thoughts and
memories effeminate infirmary
of my squandered youth
i wander in the truth
of how much better
would it be?
a cold moon and pale trees
and i'll lie here for summers
while drummers pound
out the primal patters
and battering of sins
it begins in the guts
it fucks the brain
'til the pain is a central
throbbing of stropping
sinew strobe flexing
on fleshing muscle
and bleeding bone
and now it just aggravates
like chinese water torture
how long 'til it hurts again?

Algol Von Loki

wicked dawn

balanced imbalanced
phallic fallacies and malice
alice never expected such curiousness
when she stepped through the looking glass
revolving and devolving
resolving to involve me
with all these trollops to relieve me
from sweet anger that's now a pain in the ass
i've worn myself down
these sounds resound and pound
upon soft skull tenderized
by a world unchanged
at least for the better
but i remain unfettered
relentless and embittered
but tattered battered
pale, eyes sunken
drunken and dizzied
pitied by the unenlightened
i'm frightened
not by darkness but by light
as the night cowers
from the eastern horizon
i arise in the morning
dawn comes and i die
crusted eyes try to push
past the blur and live again
but fatigue rears its ugly head
the comfort of bed
just stay dead another day
and sleep my life away

hedonistic fatalism

give me bad health
no need for stealth
when we have automation
blacken my heart
kick back and press start
recite electronic incantations
sip blood from red meat
smoke heavily and eat
fat grease sugar and salt
as my ulcer grows
my blood barely flows
my heart almost comes to a halt
caffeine nicotine
some hidden amphetamine
soaked into all
from the air to my bread
lack of sleep and liquor
to do the trick quicker
feed my id and
imbibe 'til i'm dead

Algol Von Loki

hell is people, not just other people

I'm lucid again
staring at the couch
and it's promise of exodus
what is this thing?
that marches cold,
pale, sleepless nights
ignites and alights
upon the slippery slide
down and down
we doomed careen
wild eyed sprites
who lust for the obscene
this isn't life, despair,
trust or regret
this is stagnation
do we give in? not yet
i sip stag and settle, sag
and sever slags so sweetly
watch the dead
and old gather mold
yet fold clothes so neatly
cut away the masks
and pray to spay
until i'm a single
point of awareness
fold in on myself
and disappear
but the fear
of oblivion chases me
races me through
the thousand
doors of perception
i don't want to die on earth

Garden Gnomes, Broken Bones and Catacombs

the wings of morpheus (are made of stone)

i love drugs
anti-nausea meds
mixed with nauseating
anti-pain meds
clear-my-heads and cloud-my-heads
stick-to-beds and keep-me-deads
that make me feel
so alive
slip down into
urine-warm sheets
your sun-warm beats
its syncopated rhythm
on my eurhythmic schisms
blood, grief, fear-anguish,
and lucidity
drip 'twixt my knees
and tap out
an alien tempo
most times i's hates myself
but here in my narcotic absence,
counting dwindling
neuron-stars
and forgetting why
i came and
came and
came again
soaked in shame,
necrotic sin
septic shocking
brain-dead squares
with perfectly
maligned ape hairs
troll the streets

Algol Von Loki

and alleyways
in search of saint sloth's
soma haze
and i wait, and i hide,
and the clock still ticks
and sucks the souls
of tweaked out hicks
the private dicks,
deprave-ed pricks,
prey on pristine
porc'lain priss
i pick the bones,
such sibilant hiss
spurs the serpent's
slipshod sips
i am the snake
the sloth the slave,
of morpheus,
the true, the brave
the cleansing one,
the autoclave
the one whom treated
addicts stave
poison is poison is poison
is poison. is poison
is poison is poison
is poison.
i sweat alkaline,
i breathe smoke
old heathen gods
do i invoke
and poke the fires
of pyres of sense
in the name of
entropy's defense
my nose, my veins,
my throat, my brains

Garden Gnomes, Broken Bones and Catacombs

burn like acidic
blood and feign
keto-acidosis
i befriend my psychosis
and deepen my truth
enlist the agents of gnosis
as the angels and locusts
change the angles of focus
infected blood fills a cup
in the shape of a crocus
from which
i drink life and cringe,
at the taste of death

Algol Von Loki

we love change

there was a time when
men were hard.
men were strong.
men were pricks.
they braved the wide
cold expanses of terra
with only the comforts
of lust and whiskey
to keep them company.
they stood alone.
they lived alone.
they lied to themselves.
they drank the sweet manna
that dripped from the tree
of exquisite sin
and laid prostrate
in their vomit
pining for reaping
but one day that bridge
of deceit, disdain, delusion
crashed and fell.
wryly did those
angels sing
and praised the new dawn.
for the days of
men were over.
we are anorexic.
we drink honey now
and breathe blood.

excuses of a 22 year old child

forces of nature
so esoteric and unnerving
unravel before fate-jaded eyes
and pierce, protrude, penetrate
possibly purposefully the brain
of this precariously poised pessimist
such coincidences seem
to prove the existence of
the malevolent omnipotent
deity and he writes:
"10 am thur., january..........somethin' or other,
awoke to the scowling face of my mother,
pointing at my tattered car,
hull pierced by a large uranium bar.
i point to my arm, torn, skin burned.
listen to her speeches of lessons unlearned.
roll out of bed and on to the tacks,
discarded from failed wall-hanging acts.
look at the clock and there's just enough time,
to attend reverend frizzo's temple of rhyme.
such beauty and genius and also she knows
of the artistic nature of poetry and prose.
my only hope's that she has enough class
to not point out the fact that i'm kissing her ass.
so into my car, and onto the street,
when what stands before me? a 1/2 ton of live meat!
'exodus thyself, thou bovine fiend!'
do cows even know what old english words mean?
o well, forget it, just turn around.
what i tell you next will surely astound.
throw away logic, suspend disbelief!

Algol Von Loki

for to my reverse another two sides of beef!
nothing to do but sit there and cry.
but radiation poisoning, i might die!
but just as my life starts to flash 'fore my eyes,
i'm put on a stretcher by two doctor guys.
'hurry up ya'll my life was forgetful, not great!'
as the flashes flash faster after i'm eight.
i wake up from the morphine and what's in my grip?
the leg of a cow clear up to its hip!
the radiation, with the hoof, that i held in my hand
transformed me that day into the useless cow man!
able to lactate, and stand, and eat grass,
but unable to make it on time to class."
our foil has faltered for which foils are famed;
and many more failures fall under his name.
but where's the protagonist for this poor dumb cluck?
there are no heroes for those who are fucked.

untouchable

dire straights on
the break of doom
the moon smirks back
and vile remembers
these embers of shattered lust
ravaged trust and my
passion is a cocoon
of stagnation, fornication
tastes like bile now
more gluttony to the
lips of this sick cow
i don't want to hurt
and hurt and hate my id
disgust at just what
my lower head did
i would drink the poison
of ipecac to stifle this pain
in the cold and foul reaches
of bundy's dead brain
the lame will ignite
and fire the wealth
of al capone's bones
and a dying man's health
fuck, f-u-c-k, fornication
under carnal knowledge
fornication under
consent of the king
fornication ultimately
cutaneously kevorks
can i toss this ring
and pine for its power
the guile and guilt kills
with each passing hour

Algol Von Loki

the sour taste, the consumption,
the flesh of the whale
last traces of innocence
doth ishmael impale
and kisses the sea so
at least he can drown
cursing my hubris
on the long descent down
down to dripping reaches
of distance and bite
down to poison's call,
the infinite night
will the right stifle wicked,
will the meek remain weak
will my throbbing temple
temper it's leak?

Garden Gnomes, Broken Bones and Catacombs

pt. 1: the macabre hunt

i see your face and cringe with delight
to split hairs of heiress bone
wait for safe black dark of night
and revel in the fairest moan
folded time through splayed flesh
paid in full it made my mouth
cringe and fold 'cross fishnet mesh
and follow you to your parents house
sneak slowly in with bundic glee
and bash your skull with stealthy grace
'til your visions black and you can't see
how i slice your perfect face
you're mine now bound and packaged

pt. 2: blessed pile

your entrails sprawled across the tinted glass
gleaming under fluorescent light
moist pulsing tangled mass
screaming like when ferrets fight
o my living jackson pollock
all disjointed all my own
warm gore on mangled bullock
meal of human flesh and bone
as i touch your flesh and my loins swell
head grows light pupils soar
my subconscious feigns such glorious smells
i circle as i hit the floor
and as i dream of days gone by
of the fire of lust and the fire of scorn
i picture someone's placid eye
i ask why i don't seem to mourn
all titillated with a gullet full of sick

Algol Von Loki

this sodomite man

i lie in rivers
of human sweat
swimming and suckling
on this chafed teat
of the beat and the rhythm
of the dollar's drums
the doldrums sweep by
and suck the blood of dry
mummies and zombies
the marks of the beasts
the abercrombies
the taste of
the children's toils
in oils and stench
laid expensive nothings
the uncle tom's produce
the singing dancing minstrels
blinging and sparkling
with the blood of the new niggers
as african indentured
servants cower at triggers
the figures in jew jewellers'
ledgers lean with the weight
as the new niggers tongues taste
the sting of new hate
the new rates of power,
and goddamn the poor
the whites wield their will
while the world fucks these whores
these slaves of the wage
wade 'til they drown
in starvation and aids
on the harsh desert ground
this rage is precious, and the
rest of you should be angry

the persistence of shadows

i have six-hundred sixty six reasons
to find this planet sour
count what i'm up against to infinitum
standard, status, standing
demanding omnipresence in
the sick realms of human subversion
force-fed paranoia tastes like sweat
comes back up as sarcasm and nicks
the wicks burn at both ends, the soil offends
the boils on ears and the truth can't defend
surviving just to watch it end
watch it crack and bleed
exploding and boding not for its feed
and we all are leeches vampiric sluts
the indigents sick as they lick on their cuts
fetal and watching eyelids weep not for the wicked
why won't the world turn off?

Algol Von Loki

azezel

hard eyes hollowed by hedonism
hurt and pull back
mine is a mission of entropy and chaos
sometimes with eyes closed for the tiniest second
such horrific erotic sadism
sweet succulent succubae swoon and sweat
sweep slowly sick sexual sights
across my malevolent mind
warm gooey gore, and cold gory goo
silently slip, suck, seep and sleep through
days and days of the damned demon's haze
as he tries to phrase or phase out madness
monstrously mounting mormon mother's mouths
then thrust and thrash theist thighs
lick their luscious lips, lash their legs
strap, strip and strike their flesh
tied tightly to timber, tremble, terrified
tears trickle down to be tasted on tongues
sped to the tempo of trembling lungs
exodus these thoughts or succumb to their madness

Garden Gnomes, Broken Bones and Catacombs

shooting speed

electric fried veins
the pains of these hollow gears
fears and tastes are nothing
lusting is fire in musty caverns
what are these patterns of treason
these lesions of long forgotten rotten putrid pictures
here at the fulcrum of man
pointless patterns on walls
in the halls of midwestern impression
my skin itches
this need is in my fat
souls laid in coals
weather not the soil of insolence
but chemistry is simple
and we'll fold in on nothing
these holes of souls
these trolls are the gray of solid granite
fucked by false face
of well being and emaciation
vibrate in styrene and stagnation
dying in nanoseconds
and shaking missed realization
there's god knows what in my core
fuck knows what's in store
we implore thee lord, cut the cord
i'll never make it
limping and made of sand
and melting like mist
just to aerate the land
locked in hardened heart
i hearken hoth's hand
to squeeze blood from these stones
their bones lone demand
bleeding speed feed shooting need

Algol Von Loki

cock and vial

god i love the soft warm succulent touch of your flesh.
the way you fucking saunter so sweet and cute in your
subtlety
my mind is like fire on fire
and your god if i could just touch you
taste you, wrap you in white sheets
sniff the air like it were honeysuckle
i want your blood to taste like wine
i want the sky to consume the vile wretches
but if they had time to change,
would it fucking matter.
just signing off

welling up

it's like when someone says they like you
it's like a good orgasm
it's like the fallen bearing of a goddess
it leaves you breathless
it grabs you by the throat
it makes you want to scream
god never knew such delight
fright is just a symptom of humanity
grant me amnesty
this insanity is just praise
television pixels like lice
float all grey and dusty
stink like sulphur
fair and harsh
when love is just a function of lust

the speaker

a hush fell
over the rabble
his subtle and soft
twitches won them
the shake and the
shudder of muscles
and then veins
and then molecules
and then atoms
down to the quarks
and gluey gluons
crescendo-ed and ebbed
to the hum
of the warm
gamma vibration
in the pandemic
of pandemonium
each tiny action
leads to something
as monumental as
a finger pointing
as trivial as
a supernova
played out
like chess moves
the crowd started
performing sending
off some glorious
ordered chaos
collisions like a
ballistic barrage
of bobby pins
on bowling pins

Algol Von Loki

blasting red and
white splinters of
painted wood
in their hive
core as observers
they fingered him
like an organ
"huwooo," he wheezed
and then all at once
they stopped
stopped the little
vibrations of
quarks and gluey gluons
and then atoms
and then molecules
and then veins
all the way up to muscles
all just stopped

becoming stone

holy hell! i thought
pounding on my skull
alone again in a dark hollow
insomniac amnesiac like
cyrano de bergerac
the eye-worms swivel and swerve
play tricks in the periphery
of my vision
chocolate doughnut eye sockets
and black wire hair
mouth dry from
cannabis and sleeplessness
and being unwilling
to drink water
unable to buy soda
belching sour meat
spitting nails
coughing like
a wire brush
in my throat
pissed the fuck off
giving up and tired
ready to retire
but from what?
from apathy?
from dire angry nights
spent with a backing ache
from sitting on the floor
staring deeply in a
slightly screwy television
with pale green lines
spanning its screen
retire from lazy

Algol Von Loki

days spent unemployed
from stagnation and
self-loathing
from bad pictures
of disgusting things
from chalk lines
from black spit
from paper skin
from cracked lips
from frosted tongue
from red spidery
ocular capillaries
from giving a shit
from pounding fists
from ugly despair
from tears where
there shouldn't be tears
from topical daily
comedy shows
from grinding hand cranked
drill through septum
all for the orgasmic relief
and cigarette afterward

Garden Gnomes, Broken Bones and Catacombs

バフォメイの俳句 (haiku of the baphomet)

i was just far too fucking tired to open
the first door that atlas locked,
stone dead and lucid putrid
pick the locks with bones
she was carried away flogged it was
so fucking perfect when you get exactly what you
deserved and now
i hope i don't
not now
here
!

Algol Von Loki

teetering peaks

sometimes i treat you
like one of my bookshelves
and put too much on you
but like a bookshelf
you're piled high
with the things i love
i hate to be so burdensome
but we've all been
a damned burden on
those that we love
you're hurt more by
my suffering than i am
i'm sorry that i've
hurt so much
and when the tears stream
from your face
and you tell me how
i'm wasting myself
and how wonderful
you think i am
don't think i don't feel
the guilt and the flattery
i'm starting to see
what you see
and i will do well
for myself and for you
i cried as i wrote this

lighthouse on the dark lake

it may be sapped of light
in our home and a bit
devoid of laughter but
the thing that keeps these
dark times short of
disaster is your gorgeous smile
and when you hold me tell
me everything will be
alright and when i call out to
you in the middle of the night
and from the dead of sleep
you arise to be by my side
i know your eyes red and crusted
with sleep will still smile
at me and make me feel happy
in my darkest times or when
i'm feeling crappy you brighten
my spirits and redden my
cheeks and make me feel
strong when i feel weak
i love you

Algol Von Loki

overqualified

the strain my mind should be under
falls on my back
the strain my eyes should be under
falls on my lungs
the strain my wrists and fingers should be under
at least is right where it should be
i wasn't built for this
building the things i should be designing
tearing down the things
that would still be standing were i the engineer
reading from the drawing board
rather than writing on it
what went wrong?
i know the answer
tho i don't like to say it
i pursued the inner knowledge
chose to be a psychonaut
for which no degree is offered
sailing through altered states
where there is no where
to stick a flag
to put it simply
i fucked up
but in this simple work
where the theorem of pythagorus
the square, simple division and subtraction
the tape measure and
various implements
of creation and destruction
are the only things my mind is used for
in this work i find solace and satisfaction
i find appreciation of my talents
and condemnation of my shortcomings

Garden Gnomes, Broken Bones and Catacombs

and with my command of the square
and the right triangle
perhaps the masons will call
induct me into their order
but fuck, i'm only like 1/6th irish

Algol Von Loki

mountain man soiree

the socket where
my wisdom used to be
has left just creaking
anger there and
exposed bone
blood spit pain
split head brain
fed tonguing at
the hole in
my gums as
it dries my
eyes filled with
drywall tears
and my gashed
hands ask why such
women and child
abusing cocksuckers
think they can
call themselves
manly fuck
your faggy camping
trips and your
ridiculous accusations
you can shove
your piety up
your well greased
ass you cum
guzzling pig

dewalt luck trinkets

"that foot wasn't
much luck
for the rabbit"
i thought as i spat
a wad of sawdust
onto caramel fresh
dog shit in
a rot
wood forest
my toes dug
in where my
heels shoulda
a tuning fork
jerk through
the steel bar
wrenched rust
iron joints and
disintegrated
rubber band
tendons in my
bass finger
writing finger
drawing finger
from artist to
artisan to
hunched corpse
i spill coffee
from steel carafe
i can't open
with withered
hands i think
"the monkey got
no wishes from
this paw"

Algol Von Loki

three f's

we were made all wrong
with our heart too close to our genitals
and our brain too far away
with our hair in our
armpits and buttholes
places where
it's already too hot
and our eyes
bigger than our stomach
and our ears
ugly and twisted
and buried under wax
with our bones inside
with nothing to shield us
from the wild winds
that whip into our skin
with eyelids that don't
quite block out the sun
or the memories
but for all the inefficiency
of this jumbled mess
it's how you're built
so i must confess
nature did something right
it's my function to follow your form

a limit to tolerance

a mind can only open so far
before it starts to crack at the hinges
running thick lines of megrim
around botox syringes
and the weight bears down
on a sensitive skull
and that mind starts to show
cracks in it's hull
i've learned enough from this world
the things i can tolerate
are too numerous to count
there's so much i should hate
so much i should shun
so many things i should despise
in the morning it's so hard
to open my eyes
that i'd much rather
go back to sleep
and i can't just trust things
i have no faith to leap
Reference Number 666
i'm a militant anti-militarist
a screaming ventriloquist
an immortal fatalist
and a feminist rapist
flagrantly in-flagrant
and fragrantly in-fragrant
i'm in no state i make a statement

Algol Von Loki

succubi and incubi

they eat the hearts of nice young boys
who eat the hearts of nice young girls
who eat the hearts of nice young boys
and no one gets off
in this circle jerk
they look just like us
a ginger-haired waitress
a tattoed waif
a dapper lawyer
they love the taste
of blood and souls and tears
and are immune to remorse
they are just like us
til the sun goes down
their eyes floating
in whiskey or rum
jittery jangle-armed jabberwockies
gyrate down the street
their thirst paints long shadows
on pavement wet
with the blood of virgins
and sluts alike
and i pat my chest
to see if my heart
is still there
as i look at them
with lust and adoration
appreciation for the skill
with which they strike
down the weak
my knees they quiver
and buckle as
i try to remember

the last time i felt remorse
and my mouth dries
and my eyes redden
with a thirst
for souls and blood and tears

lucifer rising

you're the hottest thing
i've ever seen on all fours
jet black punk-spangled
mess in the back
of a corpse bucket
smiling maniacally
at silvery celluloid
an east maine
crab stain
thelemite fireworks
sprinkling ink
on hot pink
soft drink
of soft lips
spill little sips
of blood from cracks
and leather burns
belial breathes
sweet sultry lullabies
through barren trees

Algol Von Loki

i meant to ask what you thought of new order

and thru some
type of unintentional
satanic magick
there stands what
you asked for
clothed in neon
and steel and ferrocyanide
and ethyl alcohol
to brave scandinavian
cold clumsy clueless
clutching country red
courage clenching
teeth and anus
and oggles with
deadpan determination
and your throat
closes clasped shut
without a friendly
hand to help
clamors gasping for
clever quips and
quick custom colloquialisms
but these stick
in your teeth
like lettuce and
popcorn kernels
and you rush inside
stymied and stifled
to reload again
and polish your rifle

Garden Gnomes, Broken Bones and Catacombs

teetotaling and anise crackers

and this basement is too dirty
and the wine stains won't come up
and the scents of rape and heartache linger
like grape grounds in the cup
but tomorrow it smells like children of bodom
and moreso in your womb
and the harsh ripping clarity
from the chemicals we consume
you look so fucking cute
with your eyes open all conscious
sober and soliloquies
will lamely lie upon us
and i know things won't be easy
a lot of it will suck
but together we can face it
without getting fucked up

Algol Von Loki

wretch in eden

we's eats and vomits and the black fishes
looks like rainbows
but not them hazy cloud things more like
bad kids art with paint colors
thick clumpy clumsy scrawled over and with
oatmeals and dry macaronies
and so we's laps water from dirty shit rivers
with clumps of animal curd
and the prickly scent of dead fishes we sniffs
but our nosehairs tingle like fresh coffee grounds
instead of the piss scent from our tattered
pants and threadbore with leaves
and when the poison seizes our muscles we knows why
the gods maked cactuses and mushrooms
do this it's to sting our tongues when shouldn't
be eating cactuses and mushrooms
and black fishes and too long dead fishes
and macaroni oatmeal paintings
it's why the gods maked water taste
sweet when we's thirsty and
clean when we's full
so it's cuz we doesn't dry out
and never too much
eats the cactuses and mushrooms and
those bitter round poppies podses
that tasteds so bitter
we's almost spit sick
it's why the gods
maked our buttholes stink
so's we wouldn't keep putting
our fingers and foods in there
but it's too late now
so churns our stomach to make
our head feel swirly and pretty clouds

and our fingers keep reaching
for black fishies we can't seem
to quit eating so tasty
and sweet now
and it's spines feels like
soft lemon pies
and we's keep choking but when
we spits the gods maked pretty
rainbow spits and we starts to think
maybe these gods is demons cuz
when we's prays they is
never come say hi but when we's dance
naked around the circled fire
they come and bow down
say what can we do?
can we make woman for you?
can we suckle you's blood?
And taste you sweet tears
and we know tears ain't sweet
we's cries enough
and they say we's smell nice
when we know the pantses is
soaked with pisses
and the say they feels us heart
and put they hands on us stomach
or the wrong sides of us chest
and we know the gods maked us so
they knows how we was maked
plus when they says
they wants to check us temp'rature
they put they hands in us pants
and they hands feels cold
but still stings and burns
so we know they no gods
but they hide they horns
and glue feathers on they wings
but we know

Algol Von Loki

they is demons that want to makes
us cries and pisses
and dries out and eats
all they icky plants
and the pretty paints full of
macaronies and oatmeals
our nieces and nephewses
workeded really hard
to make

weed and seed acquaintances

sand-blasted half-masted grey goblin
yanks crimson-coated choke collar
walks crumbling cracker streets
crackling calloused feet on cobble
clears its throat of molten magma mucous
sniffs salted cyanide scents through
snot and hair bubbling bong ripples
through watery rhinophyma
and swallows unsubstantial simalcrum
such sickly sub-sinus secretions

a faceless exotic dancer

the many-faced god
stands on the couch
and shakes it in your face
gyroscopic vibrations
but it's hard to fight the urge
to touch zor's hips
you can't touch
NEVER TOUCH!!!
TOUCHING COSTS EXTRA!!!!
but when zor poops out little goblins
that splosh down on your lap
and scramble scientology
vibrations on your junk
and you think
gods aliens or a mono-deity
but these are just the words
of ignorant humans
it's just important
to keep the conversation going...

Algol Von Loki

pasta and the operation on tlc

the first bite of spaghetti
triggered the second
which triggered the third
which triggered the so on
and the so forth
and halfway through
when i saw the maggots
swimming in the ragu
and squirming about
i was already too addicted
to stop eating
and then when
my vision cleared
and i saw that it wasn't
spaghetti at all
i was so ravenous
for the human flesh
it was revealed to be
i couldn't stop
and when i came to
the last few bites
and saw that the
flesh was moving
writhing about
and the openings of veins
and ends of entrails
were eating the maggots
that were eating it
the morbid grotesque
uroboros seemed so
succulent i just
couldn't quit eating it

Garden Gnomes, Broken Bones and Catacombs

and then i felt nauseous
but couldn't vomit
and instead the
zombified flesh
burst from my stomach
dead alive exploded from me
alien style
i still couldn't quit eating
until the entire mess
crawled from my stomach
a fully formed man
now made whole
but sans skin
and with razor sharp teeth
it unhinged its jaw
and put its mouth
around my skull
and it couldn't stop
eating me
until it was forced to pause
as its skin grew back
over its limbs and torso
around its neck
and lastly wrapping
over its face and
then i could see
that it was me

Algol Von Loki

schatzi to bijin

let the moist saline
of your pain and anguish
fall into my shoulder
in a torrent of misery
your sorrow is allowed
and accepted
it instigates
sympathy and
flattery within me
but know that it
is not necessary
for you and i are
part and parcel
of one another
they say two objects
never truly touch
that their electrons
repel one another
but with you and i
i feel the electrons part
like the red sea
and the atomic nuclei
kiss for we are
so close to one another
that our entanglement
overrides the strong
electromagnetic force
and proximity is
of no consequence
fear not being far
no worry for our

Garden Gnomes, Broken Bones and Catacombs

separation for
we are one
one and the same
part of one another
so close are you and i
so similar are we
that when we couple
it could be
incest or masturbation
and i never have believed
nor do i now
in fate or spirit or the soul
but the perfection binding
you and i
is evidence for
those things i once thought
of as esoteric metaphysical
and illogical
they are now
scientific probabilities
our hearts beat at
the same rhythm
our neurons fire
at the same frequency
we our within
one another
there is no such thing
as without each other

Algol Von Loki

fourth wall shenanigans

the eastern wall
of algol's kitchen
seemed to crumble and
dissolve simultaneously.
in its place
was a large pane
of slightly bubbled glass
through which he could see
giants sitting on
giant couches
in a giant living room.
they were rocking
back and forth and
laughing and eating popcorn.
then the backward words
started to scroll
up from the bottom
of the pane of glass
"hcnyL divaD :rotceriD"
it said, followed by
"namflE ynnaD yb cisuM" etc.
the biggest giant
lifted a mammoth
remote control from
betwixt the couch cushions,
pointed it at algol, and...

Garden Gnomes, Broken Bones and Catacombs

to the old ones you're a gas station microwavable burrito

and azathoth churns with cosmic indifference
no care for terran or human insignificance
and should a pulsing tendril enter through
an eschewed corner of your room
don't dare think there was a special care to choose you
rather he was passing through
when hunger struck him here randomly
or some cultists built a portal here in reverence
and coupled it to his realm
and mind you that's one tendril
in an infinitum of undulating plasm
that morphs and plumes in the great attractor
where space and time plunge a trillion fathom chasm
and should that tendril encircle your neck
and down your back
and up your rectum
keep in mind it could be any old flesh
tho men wish for importance, especially in death.

Algol Von Loki

About the Author

Algol Von Loki is the alter ego of writer, poet and misanthrope, Michael Brueggeman. He is a humanoid alien from another dimension where technology is organic rather than electronic. The same goes for machinery. Even Algol's house is a genetically engineered animal. This alternate dimension has its own versions of Facebook and Magic: the Gathering. On Algol's Facebook the only page he has in common with our dimension is the one that allows him to communicate with Michael. They're friends on the interdimensional social networking site, which is how they communicate ideas to one another. Algol also shares an interest in Magic: the Gathering with Michael along with their literary and artistic similarities. Algol is also an experienced pyromancer, clairvoyant, flatuery, semen-golem summoner, geomancer, bromancer, vaginomancer & technomancer (a skill he was unaware of until he spent a brief stint in our dimension).

Made in the USA
Lexington, KY
01 September 2015